AF576936

Wright & Ditson
REGULATION.
LEAGUE BALL

TAKE ME OUT TO THE BALLGAME

A BOOK OF HISTORY, HITS, AND HEROES

TAKE ME OUT TO THE BALLGAME

A BOOK OF HISTORY, HITS, AND HEROES

EDITED BY KEVIN OSBORN

ARIEL BOOKS

ANDREWS AND MCMEEL

KANSAS CITY

 For information write Andrews and McMeel, a Universal Press Syndicate Company, 4900 Main Street, Kansas City, Missouri 64112.

ISBN: 0-8362-4732-9

CONTENTS

INTRODUCTION • 7

HISTORICAL HIGHLIGHTS • 9

HEROES AND GOATS • 13

WITS AND WISECRACKERS • 23

STATISTICAL ODDITIES • 31

NICKNAMES • 35

INTRODUCTION

Baseball captures the spirit and imagination of America and Americans as no other sport does. As the historian Jacques Barzun has noted, "Whoever wants to know the heart and mind of America had better learn baseball." A sport of many paradoxes, baseball uniquely reflects the American character, culture, and ideal. Baseball, a team game played by individuals, unites people for a common purpose and then gives them the freedom to use their distinctive styles and abilities to that end. That truly is the American ideal. A democratic game, baseball allows every team member many opportunities to stand in the spotlight—to prove himself a hero or a goat.

The lines, boxes, and fences that mark the baseball field attempt to impose order on chaos—the same goal of the pioneers who settled the frontier. Yet in a complete reversal of pioneerism, baseball creates rural spaces in urban landscapes (rather than urban spaces in rural landscapes). This effort to combine country and city is also a reflection of the American ideal.

Unlike other team sports, baseball is not ruled by the clock. Baseball is timeless: a team that avoids making the third out could play forever. And the timelessness of individual games is itself wrapped in time—the progression of games day after day for six months—which allows stories to unfold in baseball as they do in no other sport. Instead of having to wait several days or even a week between games, the very next day there's another chance for success or failure.

But the true appeal of baseball, what makes it the favorite American pastime, is that it's easy enough so everyone can play the game but hard enough so few can play it well. In fact, even the pros have a fairly low success rate—the very best teams lose one out of three games. (In this century, only the 1906 Chicago Cubs lost fewer than one out of four games.) Among individuals, the success rate is even lower: the best hitters fail two out of three times!

Baseball is much like our lives: frequent setbacks and a few memorable successes. We can identify with the player who in repeated at bats strikes out, grounds weakly back to the pitcher, pops up to the catcher, and just misses a home run . . . and then, with everything on the line, drives in a double to win the game.

HISTORICAL HIGHLIGHTS

The credit for developing and recording the rules for baseball, as well as designing the modern-day baseball diamond, belongs to New York bank teller Alexander Cartwright. His rules—recorded in the charter of the New York Knickerbockers Base Ball Club in 1845—limited the defensive team to nine players on the field and put an end to the practice of throwing the ball at a base runner to put him out. Following four intrasquad games on October 21, 1845, the Knickerbockers took on the Brooklyn Base Ball Club in the first recorded game played following modern rules. The game was played across the Hudson River in New Jersey, at Hoboken's Elysian Fields. The New Yorkers handily defeated the Brooklynites 24 to 4 in this first baseball game—and then did it again with a score of 37–19 in a rematch held three days later in Brooklyn.

Baseball has survived scandal, war, and racism to become revered as the national pastime. Contrary to popular belief, the 1919 Chicago "Black Sox" scandal was neither the first nor the last time the game has been tarnished. In 1877, the National League's Louisville Grays were suspected of throwing the pennant with fifteen games to go. After an investigation, four players were banned for life and Louisville was stripped of its team. A century later, both Denny McLain and Pete Rose were banned for their association with gamblers. However, because it involved baseball's showcase event, the "Black Sox" scandal looms largest. Eight Chicago White Sox players, in return for payoffs ranging from five thousand to thirty-five thousand dollars, conspired to throw the 1919 World Series to the Cincinnati Reds. The game survived this low point largely through the efforts of two men: baseball's first commissioner, Judge Kenesaw Mountain Landis, appointed in 1921, and the game's greatest superstar, Babe Ruth.

African-American catcher Fleet Walker and his brother, Welday, were players for the American Association's Toledo Mudhens in 1884. But when player/manager Cap Anson, perhaps the biggest star of his day, refused to let his Chicago White Stockings play against teams with black players, he laid the foundation for the color barrier that would last until 1947, when Jackie Robinson became the first African-American to play in the Major League.

The first all-black team had been formed in 1885 with the first all-black league debuting in 1920. Fielding teams with names like the Kansas City Monarchs, the Birmingham Black Barons, the Homestead Grays, and the Newark Eagles, the Negro Leagues featured scores of players who could have been stars in the Major League. Shortstop John Henry Lloyd dominated the leagues until the 1930s. That decade made stars of future Hall-of-Famers Josh Gibson, Buck Leonard, Cool Papa Bell, Judy Johnson, and Satchel Paige. When the color barrier was finally broken, Paige, Roy Campanella, Larry Doby, Monte Irvin, and Minnie Minoso joined Jackie Robinson in becoming Major League stars.

HEROES AND GOATS

Although a team game, baseball puts a sharp spotlight on each individual playing it. Most plays focus attention entirely on the batter, the pitcher, and perhaps one or two fielders. This tight focus offers countless opportunities for a player to become a hero—or a goat!

HEROES

On October 8, 1956, an average Yankee pitcher named Don Larsen (81 wins and 91 losses over his career) became a star in the biggest showcase of them all. Larsen pitched the only perfect game (no runs, no hits, no walks, no errors) in World Series history.

In 1967, Carl Yazstremski almost single-handedly won the pennant for the Boston Red Sox. Yaz batted .522 with 5 homers and 16 runs batted in (RBI) over the last two weeks of the season. Still, the Red Sox trailed the Twins by one game with two to play. In the final series—against the Twins—Yaz powered the Red Sox to a sweep and the pennant by going 7 for 8 and knocking in 5 runs. His clutch performance helped Yaz become the last person to win baseball's Triple Crown.

They said the Babe's record would never be broken. Fans heaped abuse on anyone who dared challenge it. But in 1961, Roger Maris hit 61 home runs—one more than Babe Ruth had hit in 1927.

On May 26, 1959, the Pirates' Harvey Haddix pitched a perfect game, allowing no one to reach base for nine full innings. But the Braves' Lew Burdette had prevented the Pirates from scoring too. By the thirteenth inning, Burdette had scattered twelve hits without damage, while Haddix had pitched twelve innings without allowing a base runner. The only extra-inning perfect game ended when third baseman Don Hoak threw the ball away to open the thirteenth. Hank Aaron was walked intentionally, bringing Joe Adcock up to bat. Adcock homered, yet got credit for only a double when he passed Aaron in the base paths and was declared out. The heroic Haddix had lost not only the game but also the *perfect* game.

In a perfect pitching matchup, Fred Toney of the Reds and Hippo Vaughn of the Cubs held each other's team hitless through nine innings on May 2, 1917. (Vaughn gave up two hits and lost the game in the tenth.)

The last batter to hit .400 in a full season was second best in 1941's voting for the league's Most Valuable Player (MVP). In 1941 Ted Williams hit .406, the highest batting average since 1924. But that same year Joe DiMaggio had a hit in every game played for two months: 56 games from May 15 to July 16 (and then 16 more after the Indians stopped him on July 17). DiMaggio's unequaled streak and the Yankees' first-place finish won him the 1941 MVP award.

Although he could hit with some power, Bill Mazeroski was known more for his defense—until his ninth-inning homer won the seventh and final game of the 1960 World Series for the Pittsburgh Pirates.

On October 3, 1951, the Giants trailed the Dodgers 4 to 1 in the ninth inning of the final playoff game for the National League Pennant. Whitey Lockman drove in a run with a double, making the score 4 to 2 and putting the tying runs on second and third. With rookie Willie Mays on deck, Bobby Thomson drove the ball into the left-field bleachers. The stunned announcer could only chant: "The Giants win the pennant, the Giants win the pennant!"

When pitching for the California Angels in the 1970s, Nolan Ryan had led the league in strikeouts seven times and pitched four no-hitters between May 15, 1973 and June 1, 1975. But in 1979 the Angels gave up on him: Fastball pitchers tend to burn out quickly, and the Angels must have thought that at age thirty-three, Ryan was near the end of his career. Wrong: Ryan went on to pitch fourteen more seasons with the Houston Astros and the Texas Rangers. Even more amazing, he pitched his record-breaking fifth no-hitter in 1981, his sixth (at age forty-three) in 1990, and his seventh in 1991.

Pinchhitter Dusty Rhodes led the underdog New York Giants to a four-game sweep over the powerful Cleveland Indians in 1954. In the first game, Rhodes pinch-hit a game-winning three-run homer in the tenth inning. In the second game, he pinch-hit a single that tied the game and later homered for the final run in a 3 to 1 win. In the third game, Rhodes drove in 2 runs with a bases-loaded pinch single to give the Giants a 3 to 0 lead.

Despite hate mail and death threats, Hank Aaron broke Babe Ruth's "untouchable" career record in 1974. On April 8, Aaron smashed his 715th home run into the left-field bullpen in Atlanta.

Joe Carter's considerable skills had gone unnoticed for years, except by those who had seen him play in Cleveland and San Diego. However, everyone paid attention in October 1993 when his three-run ninth-inning home run against the Phillies transformed defeat into victory, winning the sixth and final game of the World Series.

GOATS

Shoeless Joe Jackson may have cheated, but he didn't do it very well. One of the 1919 Chicago "Black Sox" co-conspirators who agreed to tank the World Series, Jackson nonetheless led the Sox in batting average, runs scored, and runs batted in for the series.

The New York Giants and Chicago Cubs met in the heat of a pennant race on September 23, 1908. The

Giants (87 to 50) were just six percentage points ahead of the Cubs (90 to 53). With two outs and runners on first and third in the bottom of the ninth of a 1 to 1 tie, New York's Al Bridwell singled to drive home the winning run. As the runner scored from third, Fred Merkle—the runner at first—followed the custom of the day by leaving the field before touching second base. Cubs second baseman Johnny Evers quickly called for the ball as Giants fans streamed across the field to celebrate. The center fielder managed to get the ball back to the infield, where (after getting it back from the Giants' first-base coach, who saw what was going on and tried to pocket the ball) Evers touched the base. When the umpire called Merkle out for failing to touch second base, the winning run the Giants had scored was negated due to the "force" play. The crowds on the field and approaching darkness made it impossible to finish the game, which was declared a tie. "Merkle's boner" cost the Giants the pennant, and they finished the season tied with the Cubs for first place. When replaying the tie game that the Giants thought they had won, they lost to the Cubs, 4 to 2.

Yankee hurler Jack Chesbro set modern-day records with 48 complete games and 41 wins in 1904. A victory over the Red Sox on the final day of the season would win the pennant. Instead, Chesbro sent the winning run home on a wild pitch, giving the Red Sox the game—and the pennant.

The 1964 Phillies, in their first pennant race since 1950, held a six-and-a-half-game lead with just eleven games to play. Then they started to lose. Their manager, Gene Mauch, tried using just two starting pitchers, Jim Bunning and Chris Short, but the Phillies kept losing—and losing. They lost *ten in a row,* handing the pennant to the Cardinals.

Though hobbled by injuries, Red Sox first baseman Bill Buckner talked manager John McNamara out of replacing him defensively after the Sox scored two runs off the Mets in the top of the tenth inning of the sixth game of the 1986 World Series. A Mets comeback seemed inconceivable and Buckner wanted a chance to record the final out of the series. But after two quick outs, the Mets put three singles together for one run and then tied the game on a wild pitch. When Mookie Wilson dribbled a grounder up the first baseline, Buckner let the ball roll between his legs, giving the game to the Mets and knotting the series at three games apiece. The Mets went on to take the seventh game, and the World Series.

In game four of the 1941 World Series, the Brooklyn Dodgers led the Yankees 4 to 3 with two outs in the top of the ninth. Hugh Casey struck out Tommy Heinrich for the game's final out—but catcher Mickey Owen let the pitch get away. Heinrich reached first base on the error, Joe DiMaggio singled, and Charlie Keller doubled them both home for a 5 to 4 lead. The Yankees scored two more and shut the Bums down in the bottom half of the ninth. Instead of tying the series at two games each, the Dodgers trailed three games to one. They lost the next day too.

The Giants seemed to have the 1912 World Series won, taking a 2 to 1 lead over the Red Sox in the tenth inning of the final game. Unfortunately, in the bottom of the tenth, center fielder Fred Snodgrass dropped an easy fly ball for a two-base error. After an out and a walk, Tris Speaker hit a routine foul pop that somehow fell between first baseman Fred Merkle—yes, the same Fred Merkle as in the 1908 series—and catcher Chief Meyers. Given a second chance, Speaker singled in a run to tie the game. A sacrifice fly sent home the game- and Series-winning run for the Red Sox.

WITS AND WISECRACKERS

September is pantyhose month. No nonsense.

—Dave Parker

Overconfidence may cost the Dodgers sixth place.

—Sportswriter Edward T. Murphy, *on the hapless Brooklyn team of the 1930s.*

There are three things the average man thinks he can do better than anybody else: build a fire, run a hotel, and manage a baseball team.

—Rocky Bridges, *1950s journeyman infielder*

The space between the white lines—that's my office. That's where I conduct my business.

—Early Wynn

The secret of managing is to keep the guys who hate you away from the guys who are undecided.

—Casey Stengel

There isn't enough mustard in the world to cover that hot dog.

—Darold Knowles, *on Reggie Jackson*

Playing baseball for a living is like having a license to steal.

—Pete Rose

Fans don't boo nobodies.

—Reggie Jackson

I don't like to sound egotistical, but every time I stepped to the plate with a bat in my hands, I couldn't help but feel sorry for the pitcher.

—Rogers Hornsby

If I were playing third base and my mother were rounding third with the run that was going to beat us, I'd trip her. Oh, I'd pick her up and brush her off and say, "Sorry, Mom," but nobody beats me.

—LEO "NICE GUYS FINISH LAST" DUROCHER

I didn't come to New York to be a star. I brought my star with me.

—REGGIE JACKSON, *upon his 1977 arrival in New York*

It's designed to break your heart. The game begins in the spring, when everything else begins, and it blossoms in the summer, filling the afternoons and evenings, and then as soon as the chill rains come, it stops and leaves you to face the fall alone.

—A. Bartlett Giamatti, *1989 Commissioner of Baseball*

It's great to be young and a Yankee.

—Waite Hoyt

The best thing about baseball is that you can do something about yesterday tomorrow.

—Manny Trillo, *Phillies second baseman*

I've never taken batting practice against him and I never will. I have a family to think of.

—Bob Watson, *Astros first baseman, on teammate J. R. Richard*

When you're in a slump, it's almost as if you look out at the field and it's one big glove.

—Vance Law, *journeyman infielder*

He has a weakness for doubles.

—Bobo Newsom, *Senators pitcher, when asked if he had discovered any weak spots in Joe DiMaggio's hitting.*

How hard is hitting? You ever walk into a pitch-black room full of furniture that you've never been in before and try to walk through it without bumping into anything? Well, it's harder than that.

—Ted Kluszewski, *Reds first baseman*

It might be . . . it could be . . . it is!

—Longtime Cubs announcer Harry Caray's standard home run call

I don't want them to forget Ruth. I just want them to remember me!

—Hank Aaron

Baseball is 90 percent mental. The other half is physical.

—Yogi Berra

Our similarities are different.

—Dale Berra, *on the inevitable comparisons between him and his father, Yogi*

Ruth made a grave mistake when he gave up pitching. Working once a week, he might have lasted a long time and become a great star.

—Tris Speaker, *Indians player/manager, commenting on Babe Ruth's 1921 move to the Yankees to become an outfielder.*

The bases were drunk and I painted the black with my best yakker. But blue squeezed me, and I went full. I came back with my heater, but the stick flares one the other way and chalk flies for two bases. Three earnies! Next thing I know, skipper hooks me and I'm sipping suds with the clubby.

—Ed Lynch, *Mets pitcher, describing a baseball experience*

The good Lord was kind to me. He gave me a strong body, a good right arm, and a weak mind.

—Dizzy Dean

One day you can throw tomatoes through brick walls. The next day you can't dent a pane of glass with a rock. It hurts but you hang on, hoping it'll come back. Oh, well, it's a helluva ride, the one on the way up.

—DEAN CHANCE, *1960s Angels ace*

Here comes Roger Maris. They're standing up, waiting to see if Roger is going to hit number 61. Here's the windup . . . and the pitch to Roger . . . way outside, ball one. The fans are starting to boo—low, ball two. That one was in the dirt. And the boos get louder. Two balls, no strikes, on Roger Maris. Here's the windup . . . fastball, hit deep to right. This could be it! Way back there! Holy cow, he did it! Sixty-one home runs! They're fighting for that ball out there. Holy cow . . . another standing ovation for Roger Maris!

—PHIL RIZZUTO'S PLAY-BY-PLAY ACCOUNT OF ROGER MARIS'S 61ST HOME RUN.

F.C.

STATISTICAL ODDITIES

The pitcher with the best career winning percentage *against* the Yankees was none other than Babe Ruth. With the Red Sox, Ruth beat the Yankees 17 times and lost only 5 games for a .773 winning percentage. (Detroit's Frank Lary, known in the 1950s as the Yankee Killer, won more games (28), but also lost 13 for a winning percentage of "only" .683.)

After finishing second to Yankee second baseman Snuffy Stirnweiss in the 1945 batting race—by just .00009, the closest race for a batting title ever—Tony Cuccinello was released by the Chicago White Sox and never again batted in the Major League.

The next-closest batting race in Major League history was in 1949 when Red Sox slugger Ted Williams hit .343 (actually .3428) and finished second to Tigers third baseman George Kell at .3429. This slim margin deprived Williams (who had led the league in homers and tied for the lead in RBIs) of a third Triple Crown.

Charles "Hoss" Radbourne pitched complete games in 35 of the Providence Grays' last 37 games in 1884. He finished the season with a record-setting 60 wins and just 12 losses.

Lefty Steve Carlton went 27 to 10 with a 1.98 earned-run average (ERA) in 1972, winning almost half of the last-place Phillies' 59 victories.

Bobo Newsom, one of the few players to play through four decades (1929–1953), changed uniforms more than any other player in history. In twenty years, Newsom was signed by a team or traded to a new team seventeen times. He played with the Senators five times, the Browns three, the Athletics and Dodgers two each, and the Cubs, the Red Sox, the Tigers, the Yankees, and the Giants just once each.

The worst hitter of all time was Reds and Dodgers catcher Bill Bergen (1901–11) who hit .170 with just two home runs over an eleven-year career. Only once did his average top .200 (.227).

The worst hitter over a single season was a pitcher,

of course. Bob Buhl—a career .089 hitter—went zero for seventy in 1962, despite spending all but one game with the Cubs, who played their home games in "hitter-friendly" Wrigley Field.

In 1961, Roger Maris broke Babe Ruth's single-season home run record by knocking 61 out of the park. So pitchers probably tried to avoid pitching to Maris as much as possible, right? Wrong: Maris did not receive a single intentional walk all year! Pitchers who considered walking Maris no doubt changed their minds when they looked at the on-deck circle and saw Mickey Mantle.

Reggie Jackson struck out 2,597 times in his career—a full season's at bats (661) more than runner-up Willie Stargell.

Chicago Cubs starter Carl Lundgren had a sterling 1.17 ERA in 1907—and he still finished second to teammate Jack "the Giant Killer" Pfiester's 1.15.

Lou Gehrig—*not* Babe Ruth—hit the most career grand slams, smashing 23 home runs with the bases loaded.

The 1916 New York Giants won an incredible 26

games in a row—and still finished in fourth place for the season.

At the turn of the century, the five Delahanty brothers played in the Major Leagues (though no more than three were ever in the big leagues at the same time).

Chuck Klein drove in 170 runs in 1930—and still finished 20 runs behind league leader Hack Wilson.

On July 21, 1975, Mets second baseman Felix Millan had the most frustrating four-hit game in history. Millan singled in all four at bats; Joe Torre followed by grounding into four consecutive double plays, a National League record. "I couldn't have done it without him," Torre said of Millan.

Mickey Mantle smashed 54 home runs in 1961 and failed to lead the league! (Teammate Roger Maris hit 61.)

In 1900 Giants third baseman "Piano Legs" Hickman made 91 errors in just 118 games.

Paul Lindblad, who pitched for the Athletics, Senators, and Rangers, went eight years without making an error. The streak, (1966–74) covered 385 games.

NICKNAMES

Baseball has fostered the most colorful nicknames of any sport. Sadly, the art of the snappy sobriquet seems to have fallen into disuse. Yet the past offers us a memorable roster of names. Nicknames were derived from place of birth, ethnicity, reverence, skills (or lack of same), personality traits, physical characteristics, and animals.

Birthplace: Frankie Frisch (the Fordham Flash); Pepper Martin (the Wild Horse of the Osage); Ty Cobb (the Georgia Peach); Amos Rusie (the Hoosier Thunderbolt); Guy Bush (the Mississippi Mudcat); Red Lucas (the Nashville Narcissus); Enos Slaughter (Country)

Ethnic Nicknames: Honus Wagner (the Flying Dutchman); Lou Skizas (the Nervous Greek); Lou Novikoff (the Mad Russian); Al Hrabosky (the Mad Hungarian)

Hero Worship: Ted Williams (the Splendid Splinter); Stan (the Man) Musial; Whitey Ford (the Chairman of the Board); Carl Hubble (the Meal Ticket); Dom DiMaggio (the Little Professor); Casey Stengel (the Old Professor); Frank Howard (The Capital Punisher); Walter Johnson (the Big Train); Joe DiMaggio (the Yankee Clipper)

Batting Skills: Babe Ruth (the Sultan of Swat); Harry (Slug) Heilmann; Jimmie Wynn (the Toy Cannon); Paul and Lloyd Waner (Big Poison, Little Poison); Eddie Yost (the Walking Man)

Fielding Skills: Dick Stuart (Dr. Strangeglove); Chuck (Iron Hands) Hiller; Bob (Death to Flying Things) Ferguson

Pitching Skills: (Sudden) Sam McDowell; Al Orth (the Curveless Wonder); Walter (Boom Boom) Beck; Hugh (Losing Pitcher) Mulcahy

Personality: Frank Chance (the Peerless Leader); (Cocky) Eddie Collins; Lenny (Nails) Dykstra; Eddie Stanky (the Brat); (Smiling) Mickey Welch; (Laughing) Larry Doyle; (Silent) Mike Tiernan; Paul (Motormouth) Blair; Leo (the Lip) Durocher; Benny (Earache) Meyer; Eric (Boob) McNair; Jerome (Dizzy)

Dean; Mike (Moonman) Shannon; Bill (Spaceman) Lee; (Dim) Dom Dallessandro; Dain (Ding-a-Ling) Clay

Physique: Willie (Stretch) McCovey; Ernie (Schnozz) Lombardi; Walter (No Neck) Williams; Burleigh Grimes (Ol' Stubblebeard); Carlton (Pudge) Fisk; Frankie (Blimp) Hayes; Bob (Fatty) Fothergill; Dick Radatz (the Monster)

Animals: Fred (Chicken) Stanley; Joe (Ducky) Medwick; Rick Burleson (the Rooster); (Grasshopper) Jim Whitney; Roy (Squirrel) Sievers; Clark Griffith (the Old Fox); Harry Brecheen (the Cat); Hank (Bow Wow) Arft; Orlando Cepeda (the Baby Bull); Bill (Moose) Skowron; Jim (Catfish) Hunter

Others: Arlie Latham (the Freshest Man on Earth); John (Chewing Gum) O'Brien; Pearce Chiles (What's the Use); Tony (Poosh 'Em Up) Lazzeri; Dixie Walker (the People's Cheerce)

The text of this book was set in Melior by
Snap-Haus Graphics, Dumont NJ.

Book design by
Diane Stevenson/Snap-Haus Graphics